# Can You Tell a Tyrannosaurus from an Allosaurus?

## Buffy Silverman

Lerner Publications
Minneapolis

To JKC,
King of my heart
Love, BGS

Copyright © 2014 by Lerner Publishing Group, Inc.

All rights reserved. International copyright secured. No part of this book may be reproduced, stored in a retrieval system, or transmitted in any form or by any means — electronic, mechanical, photocopying, recording, or otherwise — without the prior written permission of Lerner Publishing Group, Inc., except for the inclusion of brief quotations in an acknowledged review.

Lerner Publications Company
A division of Lerner Publishing Group, Inc.
241 First Avenue North
Minneapolis, MN 55401 USA

For reading levels and more information, look up this title at www.lernerbooks.com.


Library of Congress Cataloging-in-Publication Data

Silverman, Buffy.
     Can you tell a tyrannosaurus from an allosaurus? / by Buffy Silverman.
        pages cm. — (Lightning bolt books™—Dinosaur look-alikes)
     Includes index.
     ISBN 978-1-4677-1355-9 (library binding : alkaline paper)
     ISBN 978-1-4677-1759-5 (eb pdf)
     1. Tyrannosaurus—Juvenile literature.  2. Allosaurus—Juvenile literature.  3. Dinosaurs—
Juvenile literature.  I. Title.
     QE862.S3S4836 2014
     567.912—dc23                                                          2013003024

Manufactured in the United States of America
2-42850-13405-8/22/2016

# Table of Contents

# Two Fingers or Three?

Millions of years ago, huge dinosaurs walked on two legs. Their arms looked tiny on their giant bodies.

Tyrannosaurus and Allosaurus were two of these giants.

Tyrannosaurus and Allosaurus were both meat eaters. Their sharp teeth and claws gripped and tore food. They belonged to a group called theropods.

Theropods stood on two legs. The birds in your yard are related to them!

They held their heads low to the ground.  Strong, short necks supported their huge heads.  Long tails balanced the weight of their heads.  But you can tell these dinosaurs apart.

Two children balance on a seesaw if they are the same weight.  A heavy tail balances a heavy head in the same way.

Count the fingers on a
Tyrannosaurus hand.
Each hand had two fingers
with hook-shaped claws.

A Tyrannosaurus
claw was about the
length of your hand.

8

Look at an Allosaurus skeleton. Allosaurus had three fingers. Its hands and claws were larger than Tyrannosaurus hands and claws.

Each finger ended in a hooked claw. Sharp, strong claws helped Allosaurus hunt.

# Finding Food

Some scientists think Tyrannosaurus was a scavenger. Scavengers find and eat dead animals. These scientists don't think Tyrannosaurus could have held live prey with only two fingers.

Animals that are hunted for food are called prey.

Other scientists think Tyrannosaurus hunted. They studied animal fossils with bite marks from Tyrannosaurus. Some of the bite marks had healed. That means an animal escaped from the hunter!

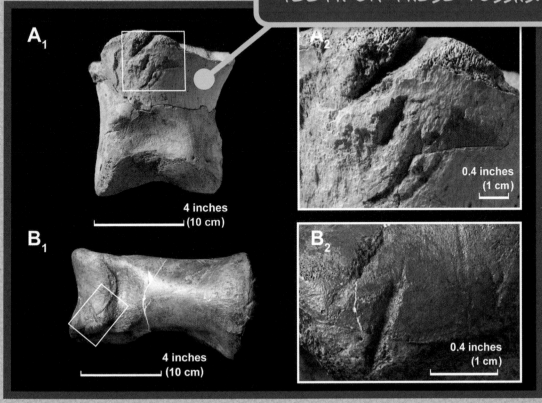

You can see bite marks from Tyrannosaurus teeth on these fossils.

A₁

A₂

4 inches (10 cm)

0.4 inches (1 cm)

B₁

B₂

4 inches (10 cm)

0.4 inches (1 cm)

# Allosaurus hunted live prey.

Scientists don't know if these dinos hunted alone or in packs. They might have battled one another for food.

Allosaurus hunted small dinosaurs. It probably hunted other larger animals too.

Allosaurus might have hunted and fought with Stegosaurus.

# Teeth: Long or Short?

Tyrannosaurus teeth were as big as bananas. They were shaped like ice-cream cones. They tore through flesh.

Allosaurus teeth were flatter and shorter. They were about the size of your fingers. Their sharp edges cut like knives.

Allosaurus could open its jaws very wide. Its top teeth worked like a hatchet. **They sliced off chunks of flesh.**

Tyrannosaurus bit much
harder than Allosaurus.
It had superstrong jaws.
Its teeth sunk deep into
flesh and crushed bones.

# Body Size: Big or Bigger?

Imagine standing on the ground and peeking into a second-story window. Allosaurus was tall enough to do that! It grew as long as a school bus.

Tyrannosaurus was even bigger. Its head could almost reach the roof of a two-story house. Its body stretched longer than Allosaurus.

Allosaurus weighed as much as a rhinoceros. Yet it was not the largest predator of its time. Other dinosaurs hunted it.

Tyrannosaurus weighed more than twice as much as Allosaurus. It weighed about as much as a large elephant. Tyrannosaurus was one of the largest land predators.

No animal hunted an adult Tyrannosaurus!

Tyrannosaurus walked on powerful legs. But it might not have been able to run. It probably moved as fast as a polar bear.

Heavy animals have a lot of weight to carry. Moving around is harder for them.

Allosaurus probably moved
faster than Tyrannosaurus.
But it did not run fast.  It might
have been
as fast as a
brown bear.

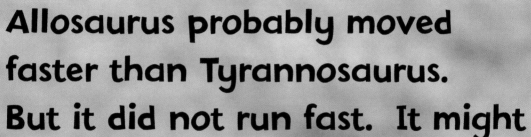

# Long Ago or Even Longer?

Allosaurus and Tyrannosaurus never met. Allosaurus lived long before Tyrannosaurus.

Allosaurus lived 155 to 150 million years ago.

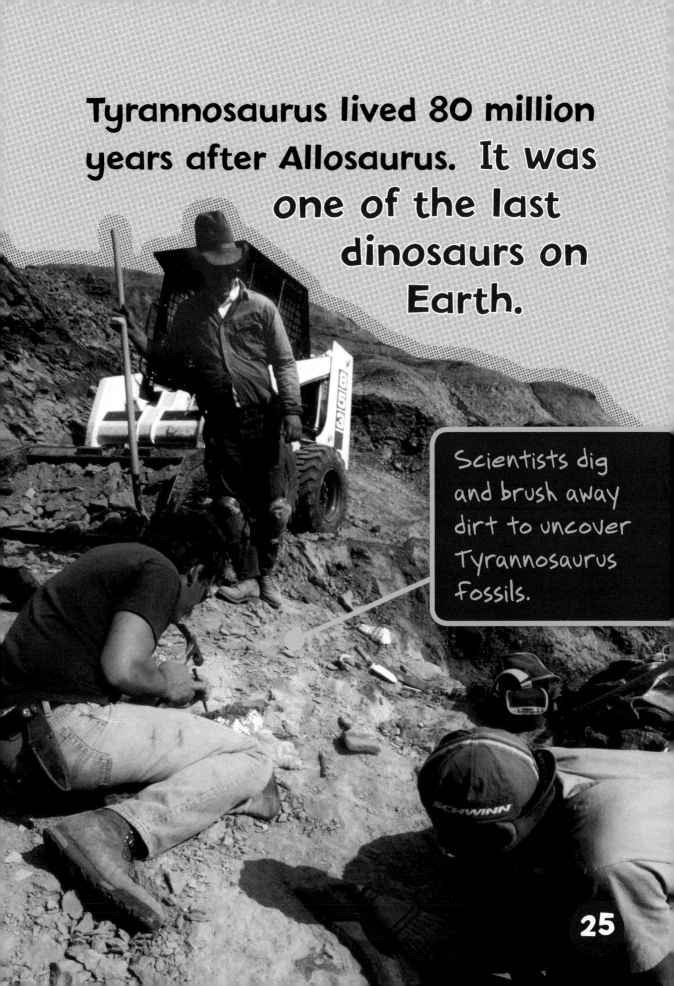

Tyrannosaurus lived 80 million years after Allosaurus. It was one of the last dinosaurs on Earth.

Scientists dig and brush away dirt to uncover Tyrannosaurus fossils.

Most Allosaurus fossils have been found in the western United States. Allosaurus also lived in Europe and Africa.

Allosaurus fossils have been found in this area of Colorado.

Tyrannosaurus roamed across western North America. People have dug many of its fossils in South Dakota and Montana. Maybe someday you will find a dino fossil!

# Dino Diagrams

## Can you tell these dinosaurs apart?

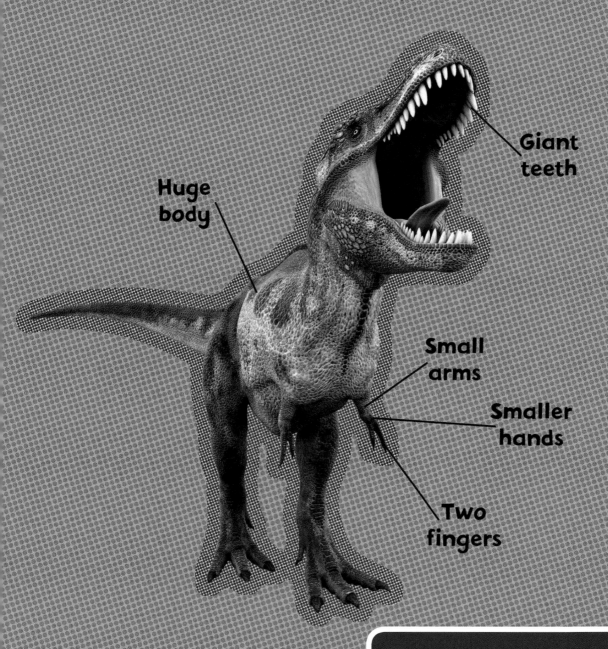

Giant teeth

Huge body

Small arms

Smaller hands

Two fingers

**Tyrannosaurus**

# Allosaurus

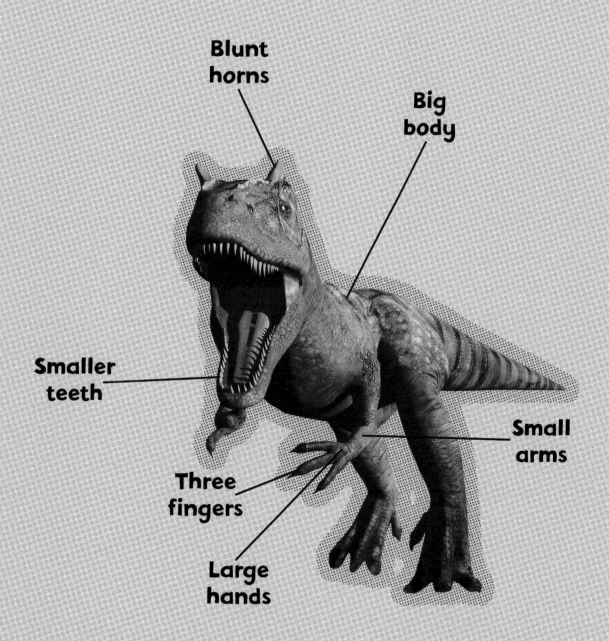

Blunt horns

Big body

Smaller teeth

Small arms

Three fingers

Large hands

# Glossary

**fossil:** the remains of a living thing from a long time ago

**predator:** an animal that hunts other animals for food

**prey:** an animal that is hunted by other animals for food

**scavenger:** an animal that feeds on dead matter

**theropod:** a member of a group of meat-eating dinosaurs that walked on their back legs and had short front arms

# Further Reading

Allosaurus Facts for Kids
http://www.sciencekids.co.nz
/sciencefacts/dinosaurs/allosaurus.html

Bacchin, Matteo, Marco Signore, and Mark Norell. *The Hunting Pack: Allosaurus.* New York: Abbeville Press, 2009.

Brecke, Nicole, and Patricia M. Stockland. *Dinosaurs and Other Prehistoric Creatures You Can Draw.* Minneapolis: Millbrook Press, 2010.

Fern, Tracey E. *Barnum's Bones: How Barnum Brown Discovered the Most Famous Dinosaur in the World.* New York: Farrar, Straus and Giroux, 2012.

Sue at the Field Museum
http://archive.fieldmuseum.org/sue

*T. rex*: The Killer Question
http://www.nhm.ac.uk/nature-online/life
/dinosaurs-other-extinct-creatures/trex-quiz

# Index

# Photo Acknowledgments

The images in this book are used with the permission of: © Andrey Troitskiy/Dreamstime.com, p. 1 (top); © Marka/SuperStock, p. 1 (bottom); © DM7/Shutterstock.com, pp. 2, 4, 28; © Eye Risk/Alamy, p. 5; © Derrick Neill/Epictura, p. 6 (left); © Ronnie Howard/Shutterstock.com, p. 6 (right); © iStockphoto.com/Stellajune3700, p. 7; © Bombaert Patrick/Shutterstock.com, p. 8; AP Photo/Monika Graff, p. 9; © Sergey Krasovskiy/Stocktrek Images/Corbis, p. 10; Courtesy Dr. Nick Longrich, p. 11; © MasPix/Alamy, p. 12; © Kayte Deioma/ZUMAPRESS.com/Alamy, p. 13; © Layne Kennedy/CORBIS, pp. 14, 25; AP Photo/Mike Derer, p. 15; © AfriPics.com/Alamy, p. 16; © Bob Orsillo/Shutterstock.com, p. 17; © iStockphoto.com/nilky, p. 18; © Rafael Ben-Ari/Chameleons Eye/Photoshot, p. 19; © Naas Rautenbach/Shutterstock.com, p. 20; © R. Gino Santa Maria/Dreamstime.com, p. 21; © iStockphoto.com/somethingway, p. 22; © Dennis Donohue/Shutterstock.com, p. 23; © Stocktrekimages RM/Mark Stevenson, p. 24; © Francois Gohier/Science Source, p. 26; © Roger Harris/Science Photo Library/CORBIS, p. 27; © Image Source/Alamy, p. 29; © Jean-Michel Girard/Shutterstock.com, p. 30.

Front Cover: © NovaStock/SuperStock (top), © Image Source/Getty Images (bottom).

Main body text set in Johann Light 30/36.